To dear Kate

with best wishes

[signature] x

ST. MARY LE STRAND DECODED

STEWART TROTTER

April 2021

ST. MARY LE STRAND DECODED

STEWART TROTTER

Published by Magic Flute Publishing Ltd. 2025
ISBN 978-1-915166-49-4
Copyright © of Stewart Trotter

Stewart Trotter has asserted his right under the Copyright, Designs and Patents Act 1988 to be identified as the author of this work.

All rights reserved. No part of this publication may be reproduced, stored in a retrieval system, or transmitted in any form or by any means, electronic, mechanical, photocopying, recording or otherwise, without the prior permission of the copyright owner.

Magic Flute Publishing Limited
231 Swanwick Lane
Southampton SO31 7GT
www.magicflutepublications.co.uk
A catalogue description of this book is available from the British Library

Photographs on pp. 37 and 59 © Katie Wignall; on pp. 38, 36 and 69 © Jianwei Chen; on pp. 44, 71 and 76 © Andrew Harris; on pp. 34 and 63 © Robin Forster. The illustration on p. 77 © Jeremy Musson.

MAGIC FLUTE
PUBLISHING

CONTENTS

The Background	1
The Architect of St. Mary le Strand	15
St Mary le Strand Church	20
Is St Mary le Strand a Jacobite Church?	32
The Evidence	32
1. The Design of the Church	52
2. The Porch.	52
3. The Winding Staircase	52
4. The Graffiti in the Stairwell.	57
5. The Inner Sanctum	60
6. The Vaults.	65
Third Degree Masonry	66
Royal Arch Masonry – The Scottish Rite	66
Postscript	78

ACKNOWLEDGMENTS

Thanks, as ever, to the great esoteric scholar, Marsha Keith Schuchard, who encouraged my researches and introduced me to Ricky Pound who shared with me his knowledge of Chiswick House. Also to my 'Investigative Team': David Kral who spotted the ouroborus on the outside East Wall and Shaun O'Brien who spotted the Rosa Alba on the ceiling.

THE BACKGROUND

First, what do we mean by Jacobite?

'Jacobus' is the Latin name for James – and the Jacobites were named after the followers of King James II who was crowned in 1685 and deposed three years later.

James II.

James I

But 'Jacobitism' itself, as a philosophy, a movement and finally a romance, goes back to 1643, the fortieth anniversary of the coronation of King James VI of Scotland as King James I of England, and the end of the first year of the English Civil Wars.

Jacobitism started life as a song – written to a 'sweet tune' to which you could march – or dance – but whose lyrics, the writer insisted, must be sung 'joyfully'. His name was Martin Parker – a hugely popular balladeer – as well as being, in his time, a vagrant, tapster, drunk and thief.

He was responding to a prediction made by John Booker, an eminent Astrologer who had successfully predicted the deaths of the Kings of Bohemia and Sweden – and was now predicting the

Charles I.

downfall of King Charles I.

Parker's ballad was originally titled 'Upon the Defacing of Whitehall' but soon became better known as 'The King shall Enjoy his own Again' or 'The King shall come Home in Peace Again'. There are variations in the lyrics – but that is hardly surprising as the song was sung for over a hundred years.

It begins:

'What Booker can prognosticate

Or speak of our Kingdom's present state?

I think myself to be as wise

As he that most looks at the skies.

My skill goes beyond the depth of a pond

Or rivers in the greatest rain

By the which I can tell that all things will be well

When the King comes home in peace again'.

Parker sets himself up in opposition to Booker – not because he has more skill in prediction but because he has more common sense. Between 1642 and the summer of 1643 there were no fewer than 14 battles between the Parliamentarians and the Royalists.

Charles I had left his Whitehall Palace and set up a base in York, but at the end of 1642 he was denied entry to London by Parliamentarian troops at Turnham Green. He set up his base in Oxford which, became a Royalist stronghold way into the eighteenth century.

Parker is saying that while the King is away from his Palace in London, there will never be peace in the land. For Parker this is not prophecy – it is fact. And by writing so directly – and vividly – in the first person, he invites you to join in with him – and become him.

The ballad continues:

'Though for a time you see White-hall

With cobwebs hanging over the wall

Instead of silk and silver brave

As formerly it used to have;

In every room, the sweet perfume,.

Delightful for that princely train;

The which you shall see, when the time it shall be

That the King comes home in peace again'.

Parker pictures the neglected Whitehall which Charles I's father, James I, had beautified with the help of Inigo Jones. Charles himself had commissioned paintings from Peter Paul Rubens, depicting King James as Solomon – the King of Peace.

The Wise Rule of James I by Rubens.

Even though Parker has been penniless at times, he enjoys the surrogate pleasure of describing King Charles surrounded by beautiful sights and smells.

> 'For forty years the Royal Crown
> Hath been his father's and his own
> And I am sure there's none but he
> Hath right to that sovereignty.

Then who better may the sceptre sway

Than he that hath such right to reign?

The hopes of your peace, for the wars will then cease

When the King enjoys his own again'.

Parker here celebrates the Divine Right of Kings which was introduced to England by James I. He believed that the monarchy was – in his own words to Parliament in 1610 – 'the most supreme thing on earth' and that 'kings are God's lieutenants sitting upon God's throne'. The King's successor should share the same blood line so that peace – not war – would follow the death of monarchs.

Oliver Cromwell was coming into prominence in 1643 when he was made a Colonel in the Parliamentarian Army.

Oliver Cromwell.

Parker foresaw his coming threat, and challenges his right to 'reign' as he is not a Stuart. The ballad, in its early version, concludes with:

'Till then upon Ararat's Hill

My hope shall cast her anchor still

Until I see some peaceful dove

Bring home that branch which I do love

Still will I wait till the waters abate

Which most disturbs my troubled brain

For I'll never rejoice till I hear the voice

That the King comes home in peace again'.

Parker refers to the story of Noah – whose ark came to rest on Mount Ararat. Like him, Parker will only know peace of mind when the dove returns with an olive branch.

Parker did not put his name to this ballad as it would have been dangerous to do so. He did, though, put his initials on one which supported the Anglican Bishops – and was threatened with jail by the Puritan Parliament.

He fell silent – but he had touched a nerve with the 'ordinary' English public. He captured their love of the Royal Family and their longing for peace.

Booker, of course, proved correct in his prediction about the decline of Charles I – even if he didn't foresee his execution. But Parker had a poetic, even spiritual, truth about his poem that was to grow with time – especially when Charles I's son, Charles II, had to flee to France. He became 'the King Over the Water' and people wanted him to fly back, like Noah's dove, to his own country.

Unknown – 17th Century.

This was to happen five years later, in 1660, when red wine flowed in the fountains of London and King Charles had a huge maypole erected where St. Mary le Strands Church now stands. The crowds at his Coronation danced round it and sang 'The King shall enjoy his own again'.

Parker, who had died four years earlier, had been accused of being a Roman Catholic because of his support for the Stuarts – and Charles I and Charles II had both married Catholic wives. Charles II converted to Roman Catholicism on his deathbed in 1685, but his brother, James, who became King James II, was by then an open follower of 'the Old Faith'.

James II wanted freedom of worship in Britain and appointed Catholics to leading positions in government and the army. This alarmed the newly formed Whig Party, who wanted to get rid of both Roman Catholicism and the Divine Right of Kings. So the King sought the support of the newly formed Tory party – and in March, 1686, the support of the Scottish Lords.

An anonymous Scottish poet wrote a poem called 'Caledonia's Farewell' to the Duke of Perth and the Duke of Queensbury, urging them to travel down to London to kiss the hands of King James to prove that 'Caledonia loves the Stuarts well'.

The poem has a strange, esoteric footnote – explaining, that because King James II was the hundred and eleventh Scottish King since Fergus, he had a right to the throne by numerology as well as blood.

The '111' can convert to an equilateral triangle which, for the 'Grecians denominated a King'. The poet added the information that the base of the triangle represented Scotland – from which the Stuart line originated – with England on the left and Ireland on the right.

The Jacobites now had a symbol as well as a song. The great esoteric scholar Marsha Keith Schuchard tells us that supporters of the Stuarts would include a triangle formed of three dots in their correspondence.

But as we can see from the medallion struck in Paris by a Masonic Lodge to commemorate Benjamin Franklin, the triangle was also a symbol of Freemasonry.

6

'Caledonia's Farewell' was published, it is thought, by a group of Edinburgh Freemasons. Certainly the poem itself praises the loyalty to the King of 'builders' and 'the cementing trade'. It also mentions Euclid and 'the Architect' – Harim Abiff – both central to Masonic philosophy and practice.

Some Masons believe that Freemasonry began in London in 1717 – but that wasn't the view of Jonathan Swift – who was friends with many of the people engaged in building St. Mary le Strand.

In the persona of 'the Grand Mistress of the Female Freemasons' Swift claims that Freemasonry started in Scotland at the time of King Fergus 'who reigned there more than two thousand years ago' and was the 'grand master' of the Kilwinning Lodge 'the antientest and purest now on earth'.

Jonathan Swift.

Masonry, the Grand Mistress claims, was first begun by Scottish Druids who worshipped – and carved – oak trees. The movement, influenced by Jewish people, developed into Rosicrucianism and 'Cabala' [Swift's spelling]. The Knights Templar later 'adorned the ancient Jewish and Pagan mystery with many religious and Christian rules'.

Stone came to replace oak as the central symbol of Freemasonry and, according to 'Swift', 'after King James VI's accession to the throne of England, he revived masonry, of which he was grand master, both in Scotland and England. It had been entirely suppressed by Queen Elizabeth, because she could not get into the secret'.

How much of this is 'literally' true is difficult to say – but a number of modern historians believe that Freemasonry did, indeed, originate in Scotland and was developed by King James VI who brought it into England in 1603.

King James's son, Charles I, attended Masonic ceremonies at Somerset House in the Strand and he too had links with the Scottish Freemasons even before the Civil Wars.

In 1638 Henry Adamson, a Scottish poet and Freemason, had

written to King Charles I asking him to repair the great stone bridge at Perth. He predicted to his fellow Masons:

'Therefore I courage take, and hope to see

A bridge yet built although I aged be'.

He then explains to his brothers why he is so certain this will happen:

'For we be brethren of the Rosie Crosse

We have the Mason Word, and second sight,

Things for to come we can foretell aright,

And shall we show what misterie we mean

In fair acrostics 'Carolus Rex' is seen.

Describ'd upon that bridge in perfect gold…'

'Carolus Rex' is King Charles I – and it has been suggested that the acrostic reads 'Roseal cross' – a reference to Rosicrucianism.

Etienne Morin, an eighteenth century French sea-faring trader and leading Freemason, claimed that Charles I's son, Charles II, also had links with the Freemasons in Europe and formed Masonic Lodges in France when he was in exile.

Another eighteenth century Freemason, Nicholas de Bonville, also suggested that a network of Freemasons – led by Colonel George Monck (who was said to have converted from the Parliamentary Army to Freemasonry in Scotland) engineered King Charles II's Restoration to the British Throne.

We know from papers left by Thomas Hearne, the Jacobite underkeeper of the Bodleian Library, that Charles II, when in exile, adopted for his personal symbol the ouroboros – the snake that feeds on itself.

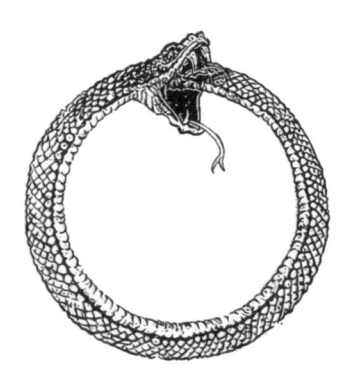

This symbolised the immortality of the Stuart line and its constant return, but it was also associated with Freemasonry and Rosicrucianism, as we can see when we look at the Franklin Medal again, where it symbolises Craft ideas of renewal and rebirth.

Another symbol emerged at the Restoration which was linked to both Freemasonry and the Stuarts was the oak tree – worshipped by the Druids – which came to represent Charles I – chopped down by Cromwell.

Saplings, though, spring from the oak tree, which represent Charles I's sons, Charles II and James II.

Charles II also famously hid in an oak tree, disguised as a peasant, after his defeat at the Battle of Worcester.

The idea grew that he took on himself the power and fertility of the oak – which loses its leaves in winter but regains them in summer.

A contemporary drawing showing Prince Charles hiding in an oak tree.

He became associated with fruit and flowers, pomegranates and grapes – and all the joys of spring. Charles II is celebrated as the Garland King or Green Man on Oak Apple Day in parts of England up to present times.

Charles II's wife – Catharine of Breganza – was unable to bear children, but Charles himself was certainly fecund: he fathered at least

Oak Apple Day, 29th May.

fourteen of them outside his marriage, two with the beautiful Nell Gwn...

Charles's brother James II managed to produce a son with his wife, Mary of Modena in 1688 – also named James. James II's daughters, Mary and Anne, were both Protestants, but now he had a son, Whigs feared it would be the start of a Roman Catholic dynasty. King James's enemies put it around that the baby boy had been smuggled into the Queen's bedchamber in a bedpan.

Seven notables – including aristocrats and the Bishop of London – invited the Calvinist William of Orange – who was married to King James II's daughter Mary – to invade Britain.

King James was arrested, but escaped from his Dutch guards and fled abroad.

Loyalist Jacobites rose up in Ireland and Scotland, but King William and the Government Army defeated them. The Scottish Highland Jacobites – under John Graham of Claverhouse – known as 'Bonnie Dundee' – had a famous victory at Killiekrankie, but Dundee himself was shot and killed in the battle.

Political songs started up again and many Jacobite scholars believe that 'God save the King' began life as a Jacobite anthem. It existed in a Latin form sung in James II's Catholic Chapel in Whitehall and its lyrics,

Catherine of Braganza.

William of Orange.

John Graham.

especially 'Send him victorious', sound as though they are addressed to a 'King over the Water'. The anthem – which is also engraved on Jacobite drinking glasses….

…..has the phrase 'Soon to reign over us' and asks God to bless 'The True Born Prince of Wales' – which sounds like a reply to the bedpan scandal.

The song goes on to bless what is clearly the Roman Catholic Church and hopes that it will remain….

    'Pure and against all heresy

    And Whigs' hypocrisy

    Who strive maliciously

    Her to defame'.

The last verse runs….

    'God bless the subjects all,

And save both great and small
In every station.
That will bring home the King,
Who hath best right to reign
It is the only thing
Can save the Nation'.

This is a re-run of 'The King shall enjoy his own again' – which the Irish Jacobites were still marching to in the 1690s and which the Bristol Jacobites were still dancing to when Queen Mary died in 1694...

James II died in exile in 1701. The Pope in Rome immediately acknowledged James's son as 'King James III'....

James, eldest son of James II.

.......but in London the Act of Settlement was passed the same year which decreed that only a Protestant could become King or Queen of England.

King William died the following year – following a fall from his horse which had stumbled over a molehill. The Jacobites had a new coded toast: 'To the little gentleman in the black velvet waistcoat.'

James II's younger daughter, Anne, a High Church Anglican,

became Queen of England.

Loyalists hoped that Queen Anne and her husband, Prince George of Denmark, would produce heirs to secure the Stuart line – but though Anne had 18 pregnancies, none of her children survived.

When Prince George died in 1708, it became clear to everyone

Queen Anne reigned from 1702-1714

that Anne – then 43 – would have to nominate her successor. She was rumoured to favour her half-brother, James III, known as 'The Pretender' to his enemies.

Most of the Tories also backed James III and tried to persuade him to become a Protestant.

The Whig Party, however, favoured Sophia of Hanover, but she was approaching 80. Failing her, they would invite George Louis, the Elector of Hanover, to become King of Britian.

He was 54th in line to the throne, but a Protestant.

It was now a waiting game to see who Queen Anne would nominate in her will.

Meanwhile, Militia Men marched through the City of London in 1711 – to the tune of 'The King shall enjoy his own again'....

King George I.

THE ARCHITECT OF ST. MARY LE STRAND

James Gibbs was seven years old when Bonnie Dundee was killed at Killiecrankie. He was born in Aberdeen to Roman Catholic parents who continued to practice their faith, even though it had been banned in Scotland. Young James was a devout Catholic – so devout he determined to go to Rome to train as a renegade priest. When Gibbs's parents died, around 1700, he sold their isolated home to the Aberdeen Freemasons to use as a Lodge.

There had been Lodges in Aberdeen since the beginning of the sixteenth century – but they had been for working Stonemasons – and were like early Trades Union. Many of the Masons were unlettered – so rote-learning took the place of books, and handshakes and passwords took the place of certificates of proof of training. These were called Operative Lodges.

But in 1670 a Speculative Lodge was established in Aberdeen for those not in the building trade but interested in the history and philosophy of Masonry – and eager to embark on its course of self-improvement and enlightenment. All that was required was a nomination, a wish to enter a supportive brotherhood and a belief in a Supreme Architect of the Universe. So Jewish people, Roman Catholics and even Quakers, were welcome as Brothers to the Aberdeen Lodge.

Gibbs was a Freemason: James Anderson in his 'Constitutions of the Freemasons' describes him as 'Bro. Gib' and describes him walking in a Masonic procession in 1721 to the 'levelling' ceremony at St. Martin-in-the-Fields Church. It is perfectly possible Gibbs's father was a Mason and that Gibbs, then 18, was 'fast-tracked' into the Aberdeen Lodge before he left for Rome.

We know that on the way there he visited Paris and may well have introduced himself to the exiled Catholic Stuart family. But when he arrived at Rome, he was so terrified of the Italian Jesuit who ran the Scots College that he left without taking his oath. He became apprenticed to some of the top architects in Rome, including Carlo Fontana, sold his water colours to aristocrats on their Grand Tour and acted as a guide.

Word reached him that his half-brother was dying, so he returned to Scotland in 1709 – but arrived too late. There was no money for him in his native country – so he journeyed down to England.

But there was no money for him there, either.

For 'four years he starved' and wrote that he had 'a great many very good friends here … of the first rank and quality … but their promises are not a present relief for my circumstances.'

But being 'of good parts and virtuously inclined and well disposed'…….

James Gibbs (left), and John Erskine, Earl of Mar (above)

……Gibbs was lucky enough to catch the eye of John Erskine, 23rd Earl of Mar – a fellow Scottish Freemason and architect – who was in London working on the Union between England and Scotland.

Mar called Gibbs 'Signor Gibbi', gave him some minor architectural work in Alloa in Scotland and appointed him Surveyor of Stirling Castle. The money for Gibbs's Surveyorship soon ran out.

But Mar had another idea….

Two years after Gibbs came to England, there had been a massive power shift at Queen Anne's Court. The Queen had fallen out with her friend, Sarah Churchill, an ardent Whig.

So the Tories were back in power.

They came up with a plan to build fifty new churches, in the High Church Anglican style, in the suburbs of the City of London – to celebrate the piety and power of the Stuart dynasty. Queen Anne – like all the Stuarts – loved architecture – and gave her full backing to the scheme.

Mar introduced Gibbs to Sir Christopher Wren, who was then in his late 70s.

A Tory (he sat as an M.P. in the Loyal Parliament to support James II), a Jacobite (he had been Surveyor of the King's Works to Charles II) and a Freemason (to this day his gavel is on show at the Museum of Freemasonry in London), he became 'much Gibbs' friend and pleased

Sir Christopher Wren.

with his drawings'. Wren and Mar came up with a scheme to make Gibbs one of the two surveyors on the Commission for Building 50 Churches.

But there was a problem. John Vanbrugh, the playwright and architect, was on the Commission as well….

……and he and Wren hated each other. Vanbrugh was also a Freemason – but he was a Hanoverian Freemason. An irrevocable split had begun in the Brotherhood…..

Sir John Vanbrugh.

Vanbrugh supported a different candidate for the Surveyor's post – John James – ten years older than Gibbs and with a lot more experience. Wren and Mar had to call on the help of Queen Anne's proto-Prime Minister, Lord Harley (Tory, Jacobite and Freemason) her Chancellor of the Exchequer, Robert Benson – newly created Lord Bingley (Tory, Jacobite and Freemason) and even her Physician, Dr. Arbuthnot (Tory, Jacobite and Freemason) to push the appointment through....

ST MARY LE STRAND CHURCH

By 1714 the Maypole that Charles II had erected in the Strand had fallen into disrepair and the Commission decided to replace it with a church – St. Mary le Strand. It would be on the Processional Route from Westminster to St. Paul's Cathedral and Queen Anne loved processions.

The Church would also raise the tone of the area which had become a notorious red light district since the Restoration.

It was planned to place a statue of Queen Anne over the Church's porch. But the Jacobites on the Commission came up with an even more striking idea. A huge column – like Trajan's Column in Rome – even higher than Wren's Monument to the Great Fire – with an internal spiral staircase and viewing platform, four guardian lions round the base, and a statue of Queen Anne at the top.

Gibbs, who had submitted a design for the Church, but had lost out to Thomas Archer, was given the consolation prize of designing the column.

But the Queen's health, which had never been good, was getting worse. By 8th July it was so bad the Commission considered a six week adjournment. On 15th July a Committee was set up 'to confer together' about the design of the Strand Church. If the Queen died, everything would change.

The Commission, though, took a chance and went ahead with the column. But on 1st August, 1714 the Queen did die.

Intestate.

Four days later work on the column was stopped, and everyone started to plot.

The Tory Party at the time was hopelessly divided, so the Whigs swept back into power. Sophia of Hanover had died a few weeks earlier, at the age of 83, so the Elector of Hanover was proclaimed King George I of Britain, France and Ireland.

To the Jacobites, of course, this was a catastrophe. Loyalty to the Stuart Family suddenly became treason. If you drank a toast to 'James III' you could be put in jail for two years. One poor soldier knelt as he toasted the 'King over the Water' and was flogged to death.

Secret Jacobite symbols had to be employed all over again – and new songs written – collected by James Hogg and published in two volumes in 1819 and 1821. Hogg – 'the Ettrick Shepherd', who really had been a farm worker before he turned writer – is not always reliable and may even have forged some of the songs himself. But many are contemporary – and even those written later – when Jacobitism became a remembered romance rather than a movement – give us an insight into what people were thinking and feeling at the time.

James Hogg.

'The Blackbird', though, which Hogg describes as 'a street song of the day' is genuinely contemporary:

In this a 'fair lady' sobs and laments the loss of her 'blackbird' – the code-word for James III who had a swarthy complexion and dark hair – like Charles II who was called 'The Black Boy' by his mother. A Spanish gene seems to have been introduced to the Stuart family by Charles II's maternal grandmother, Marie de Medici….

Marie di Medici.

'My blackbird for ever is flown.

He's all my heart's treasure, my joy and my pleasure,

So justly, my love, my heart follows thee;

And I am resolved, in foul or fair weather

To seek out my blackbird, wherever he be.'

Britain, in many Jacobite songs, became a woman, yearning for her beloved bird – in the way Parker had yearned for the return of the dove of peace.

Scottish Jacobites were particularly scathing about King George I. In 'The Wee Wee German Lairdie', a song in almost impenetrable dialect, the Scots display contempt for the new monarch, not only because he is small, but because, when word came to him that he was King of England, he was found hoeing turnips in his garden.

And though he was the King of England, he could not speak English...

'The very dogs o' England's court

They bark and howl in German'.

If he ever tries to enter Scotland 'our Scots thristle [thistle] will jag [prick] his bum'.

In another Jacobite song, 'At Auchindown', George I is described as 'cuckold Geordie' and in 'Jamie the Rover' there is a reference to the King's 'horns':

'In London there's a huge black bull

That would devour us at his will

We'll twist his horns out of his skull

And drive the old rogue to Hanover'.

George I's wife, Sophia Dorothea of Celle, had been accused of having an affair with Count Philip Christoph von Konigsmark. The Count went missing – murdered, it was rumoured by George, who locked up his wife at the Castle of Ahiden.

She took her revenge by always referring to him as 'Hagenschnaut' – 'Pig Snout'.

George was crowned on 20th October 1714 – provoking Jacobite riots in twenty difffrent English towns....

A fortnight later, a meeting of the Building Committee of the Commission for Building 50 Churches convened, chaired by Lord Bingley and composed of Dr. Arbuthnot, Sir Christopher Wren and his son (also called Christopher and also a Tory, a Jacobite and a Freemason).

Vanbrugh (newly knighted by King George and with Blenheim Palace to his credit) and Gibbs (only 30 and without a single public building to his name) 'both laid before the committee two designs for the next church 'to be erected near the Maypole in the Strand'. The committee judged both designs were 'proper to be put into execution' and 'referred to Commissioners to make the choice.

At this point two pages have been ripped out of the Minutes book of the Building Committee...

Two days later the designs were submitted to the Commission itself – who, as usual, voted by secret ballot. Wren was not in attendance – but his son was.

Gibbs was awarded the commission. The Jacobites had won.

But Gibbs nearly lost the job. His mentor, the Earl of Mar, was the leading Jacobite in Britain and he led the Jacobite Rebellion of 1715.

It failed, of course, but it introduced the most powerful Jacobite symbol of all - the five-petalled White Rose.

According to Hogg, there was a gathering of Northern Jacobite men and women at the ruined Auchindown Castle in Scotland on 10th June, 1715 – the anniversary of James III's birthday.

The Castle had been the temporary headquarters of Bonnie Dundee during the 1689 Rebellion, so the Jacobites met there to drink to the memory of Dundee and the health of James III.

Auchindown Castle.

They picked wild, white alba roses......

......then pinned them to their bosoms and bonnets and danced.

'Of all the days that's in the year

The tenth of June I hold most dear,

When our white roses all appear

For the sake of Jamie the Rover.

In tartans braw our lads are drest

With roses glancing on the breast

For among them a' we love him best,

Young Jamie they call the Rover.'

Legend has it that the Earl of Mar's Jacobite soldiers wore white ribbons in their bonnets, shaped into roses.

The famous 'White Cockade' had been born.

The White Cockade.

'My love was born in Aberdeen,

The bonniest lad that e'er was seen,

But now he makes our heart fu' sad

He's ta'en the field with his white cockade.

O he's a ranting roving blade!

O he's a brisk and bonny lad!

Betide what may my heart is glad

To see my lad with his white cockade!'

The Earl of Mar fled from Britain at the end of 1715 and at the beginning of 1716 all the suspected Jacobites were thrown off the Commission for Building 50 Churches – including Wren, Arbuthnot, Bingley and Gibbs.

A rival Scottish architect called Colen Campbell had written anonymously to the Commission, accusing Gibbs of being a 'Papist' and a 'disaffected person'. Gibbs was sacked as the Commission's Surveyor and taken off the St. Mary le Strand project.

Gibbs of course denied the charges – which were completely true – and made the Commission an astonishing proposal. He would design and build the Church for nothing. His only condition was to take his designs away with him – 'and no-one be allowed to take a copy…. he intending to engrave it for his own use'.

This was an offer the Commission could not refuse. King George had no interest in architecture – certainly not Anglican architecture – and the Commission wanted to wrap up the fifty church project as quickly and as cheaply as possible.

But they came to regret their decision. It meant they could not check that Gibbs was following the designs they had agreed to and, because they were not paying him, they could not control him.

Gibbs was also in a secret, coded correspondence with the exiled Earl of Mar. It is clear from the letters that Gibbs was working as a Jacobite agent – using codewords like 'landlady' for King James III and 'Benjamin Bing' for Robert Benson, Lord Bingley.

Mar wrote to Gibbs on 16th April 1716 that 'Benjamin Bing in Westminster now ought to build the lodge for himself or someone else' [using 'building the lodge' as a code for recruiting Jacobites] and hopes 'it may come to be built upon the bank where it was designed' [i.e. take over the running of Parliament in Westminster].

At this point Gibbs was even planning to join Mar in France.

Dislike of Hanoverian rule was growing in London and all the rest of the country. People feared a Lutheran King would bring back the bad old days of Cromwell.

There were two flash points in the year: the first was 29th May, Restoration Day, when King Charles II had returned to England from exile. People now wore sprays of oak leaves, decorated their front doors with oak boughs and danced round oak trees and maypoles.

> 'The lads took heart, and dressed themselves
> In rural garments gay
> And round about like fairy elves,
> They danced the live-long day;

Around around an oaken tree
They danced with joy, and so do we.'

The educated Jacobites would paint their oak boughs gold – in memory of Aeneas who plucked a golden bough from a tree so he could enter the underworld.

Jacobites identified the exiled Aeneas with James III – hoping that in the way Aeneas founded Rome, James would found a new Augustan Age when he was back in Britain..

The Freemasons also hoped he would bring back the fashion for building in stone. Protestant Kings favoured brick…

The second flashpoint was the 10th June – James III's birthday, White Rose Day – when people carried and wore bunches of white roses.

Soldiers went through London, snatching oak leaves and roses from the people and arresting those who resisted. But all over the country people made fun of George I by brandishing turnips and wearing horns on their heads.

And, of course, everyone was still dancing and singing to 'The King shall enjoy his own again'…

In November 1718 the Commission Surveyors got suspicious and visited the St. Mary le Strand building site. They were horrified by what they saw and recommended to the Commission that 'a stop should be put to the extravagant carvings within the Church'.

In March the following year the Commission resolved that 'Before Gibbs direct any further carvers' or painters' work for finishing Strand Church design and estimate to be laid before Board so that agreement may be made with artificers before they are put in hand. Copy to Gibbs'.

But Gibbs was off. Word had got round about the beauty of St. Mary le Strand, as Gibbs predicted it would, and work came flooding in. Interestingly he had been employed by Lord Burlington at Chiswick House, but Burlington diplomatically 'sacked' him when he was accused of Jacobitism. The reason for this – as Jane Clark, and later Ricky Pound, have argued – is that Burlington – seemingly a pillar of the Hanoverian Establishment – was in fact a closet Jacobite.

In a letter to King James III in October, 1719, the Earl of Mar compares the exiled Stuarts to the exiled Israelites and hopes that King George I – like Cyrus the Great of Persia who invited the Israelites to

The Earl of Burlington.

return and rebuild the Temple of Solomon – will invite the Stuarts to return to Britain.

Clark believes that Chiswick House was a Jacobite Temple – dedicated to the return of the Stuarts. It is full of discreet Jacobite symbols – discreet because they had to be...

One of mantlepieces (shown on p. 29) has a King Charles II Green Man; another has thistles, and roses, and grapes and fleur de lyses.

The reason for the fleur de lyses is that, at the end of 1720, James III and his wife, Maria Clementina Sobieska, had a son, Charles Edward Louis John Casimir Sylvester Severino Maria Stuart – better known

29

to the world as 'Bonnie Prince Charlie'. At birth he was created the Prince of Wales and inducted into the Order of the Thistle. Jacobite astronomers claimed that a new star had appeared in the sky.

Charles Edward, 'Bonnie Prince Charlie.'

Now there was a distinct hope of a Stuart dynasty – and Chiswick House is full of the faces and bodies of putti and young men and women, encouraging Stuart procreation.

Some of them seem to have fleur de lyses in their hair…

And as we have seen, Freemasonry went hand in hand with Jacobitism from the very beginning.

Chiswick House has a blue velvet room, a colour associated with 'Cabala' Masonry (now called Third Degree Masonry) and a red velvet room, a colour associated with Knights Templar Masonry (now called Royal Arch Masonry).

Chiswick House is separated from the main family dwelling. It has no kitchen – but it does have a wine cellar and a spiral stairway – ideal conditions, Jane Clark argues, for Masonic Rites – designed to will the King over the Water back to England.

Could any of this apply to St. Mary le Strand?

IS ST MARY LE STRAND A JACOBITE CHURCH?

OR EVEN A MASONIC ONE?

THE EVIDENCE

It has often been said that if you fell asleep and woke up in St. Mary le Strand, you would think you were in Rome.

What is remarkable is that the Church was consecrated in 1724 – ten years into the reign of a Lutheran King.

Many of the people on the Commission for Building 50 Churches were Jacobites and must have known what Gibbs was going to design. And as Gibbs was given the commission AFTER the Coronation of George I, it is hard not to see the building of St. Mary le Strand as an act of subversion.

Gibbs liked to live dangerously. In the introduction to his 1728 book on architecture he wrote:

'Designs should not be altered by the caprice of ignorant, assuming Pretenders.'

Anyone with the slightest knowledge of Gibbs would know by 'Pretenders' he wasn't referring to James III and Bonnie Prince Charlie – he was referring to what were for him the real 'Pretenders', Kings George I and George II – or Dunce the First and Dunce the Second – as Gibbs's great friend, Alexander Pope, called them.

Also Gibbs was a Scottish Freemason and, as we have seen, Freemasonry there was associated with second sight. Swift's 'Grand Mistress of the Female Masons' goes even further to suggest that Scottish Freemasons were thought to be 'conjurers and magicians'.

By creating a 'Roman Catholic' church, was Gibbs willing Roman Catholicism back into the country – and with it James III?

Gibbs remained a Catholic and Jacobite all his life. He took the Last Rites and left money for a Mass to be said for him on his death.

The bust of Pope which Gibbs commissioned and was found in Gibbs's house after Gibbs's death.

The most striking feature of St. Mary le Strand is its ceiling, filled with white flowers.....

But if you look closer you can see oak leaves and fruits....

And if you look closer still, the five leaf rosa alba....

....the inspiration for the White Cockade.

Chrysostom Wilkins plastered the ceiling to Gibbs's design in 1718 – the very year white roses were banned from London.

The walls of the church were left blank....

35

......but clearly Gibbs hoped they would one day be painted – as they were in the chapel of Wimpole Hall which he designed for Edward Harley, 2nd Earl of Oxford....

Perhaps the subject would have been 'King Solomon' – in honour of King James VI and I, 'The Scottish Solomon' – or the 'Return of the Israelites to Israel' – pre-figuring the return of the Stuarts....

Perhaps even celebrating it.

On 17th March 1720 the Commission for Building 50 Churches demanded to see the design for the pulpit – and they were right to do so. Not only is it oak – a subversive act in itself – it is covered with carvings of oak leaves, with little faces peeping through them – like re-incarnations of King Charles II hiding in the tree.

Bonnie Prince Charlie was still a toddler when these putti were carved.

If we move to the apse we see a bird flying towards us – and we experience Parker's Civil War ballad, carved in stone.

It is Noah's dove of peace returning to England.

…..as it does on Jacobite drinking glasses….

But it is also the Blackbird – James III – flying back to his home, surrounded by luscious fruits and grapes – symbols of the Stuart fertility.

There are starbursts in the apse – suggestive of the star that appeared at the birth of Bonnie Prince Charlie….

And the putti here – and indeed – all over the Church – have wings that – as at Chiswick House – could be taken for the ostrich feathers of the Prince of Wales.

Gibbs also went in for caricature – the equivalent in plaster and stone of the 'Wee, wee German Lairdie' song.

As the putti get higher and more out of sight…

……..they get more grotesque…..

……..and even demonic…

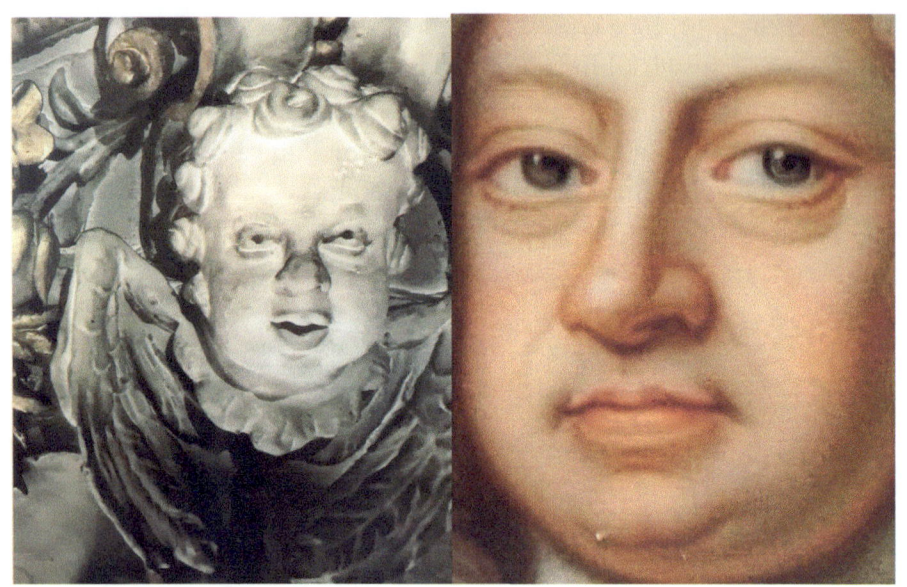

…….and start to look more and more like 'Pig Snout'!

And even the Hanoverian crest isn't all it seems to be.

If you look closely at the unicorn you'll see it has a massive horn – a mocking reference to 'cuckold Geordie'.

And it even has Stuart oak leaves carved into it….

But the real mystery are the two pillars that lead into the Church Garden.

They were not part of the original design and seem to have appeared around 1740. There is no record of the church having paid for them – so they seem to be a gift….

In 1740 Bonnie Prince Charlie was 20 – and the Jacobites were hoping he would lead another rebellion. They were even sending him tartan trews and a sword and buckler.

The piers show more putti with Prince of Wales feathers round them – and even disguised 'saltires' – St. Andrew's Cross - at the same angle as Gibbs designed a house for the Earl of Mar in Scotland.

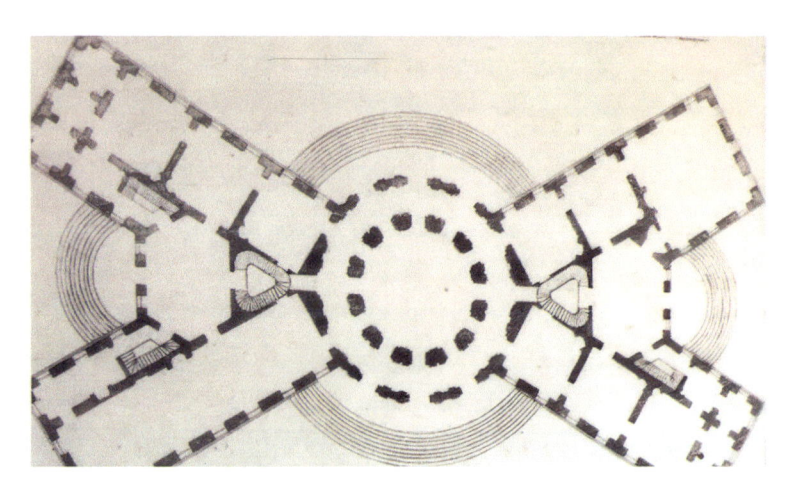

There are even thistles….then banned in England….

……but carved upside down, pretending to be tasells!

If you look for them, you can even find five petal Jacobite roses…..

Were these a 'magic' enticement to Bonnie Prince Charlie to make a bid for the British throne?

All of the elements on these pillars add up to the insignia of 'The Order of the Thistle' – given to Bonnie Prince Charlie the day he was born – and this is said to be the flash he wore at Culloden….

Who paid for these pillars? And, it must be asked, who really paid for the Church?

Officially the Hanoverian Commisioners – who on 26 January 1721 were demanding 'plain and cheap carving' for Deptford Church – finally paid a total of £17,000 for St. Mary le Strand – the equivalent of just over £4 million in today's money.

It has recently been estimated that to replace St. Mary le Strand today – with all its elaborate stone carving – would cost around £32 million.

Who had the equivalent of that sort of money in the 1720s?

Is the answer carved high up on the outside East wall of the Church?

44

Here we can see, if we know what we're looking for (and our eyesight is good enough!) an ouroboros again – with the background of a 'V'.

Is this a reference to the Jacobite 'National Anthem'? 'Send him Victorious'?

The ouroboros – as well as being the symbol of Charles II and the Freemasons – was the symbol of a Jacobite group on the Welsh border called the 'Cycle of the White Rose' Club' – who struck a commemorative medal in 1780.

This Club – which also campaigned for the abolition of slavery – was quasi-Masonic, with codewords and secret handshakes, but met in each others houses around Wrexham. Their habit was to toast the 'King over the Water' by standing with one foot on a chair, another on the table, and holding their glasses of claret over a massive bowl of rosewater.

The Tories drank claret because it was from France, while the Whigs drank port, because it was not.

Unmarried women – accompanied by a companion – were sometimes invited to meetings, perhaps in a long-term bid to boost numbers…

The club – consisting mostly of landed gentry – was run by a Welsh Tory land-owner of such fabulous wealth he was called 'The Prince of Wales' – Sir Watkin Williams-Wynn. He died in a fall from his horse, leaving debts of £120,000 – the equivalent today of £34 million.

Here he is shown wearing the 'True Blue' of a Tory.

He was also an M.P. – so he was often in London – and, like Burlington, financed the Jacobite Rebellion. He secretly organised Jacobite riots, but publicly burnt a portrait of George I in 1722. In 1740 he even offered to help finance the French Army if they were to invade Britain with Bonnie Prince Charlie.

Like Lord Burlington, he was a double agent. At the same time as serving in Henry Pelham's ministry, he secretly travelled to Versasilles to plot with King Louis XV – even though France and England were at war at the time.

Sir Watkin was a devout, High Church Anglican who would have loved Gibbs's work on St. Mary le Strand.

He was also a great friend of William King – the Jacobite Master of St. Mary's College, Oxford – who in turn was one of Gibbs's closest friends. King and Gibbs later created the Radcliffe Library in Oxford – and Sir Watkin Williams acted as their Trustee.

In 1719 Sir Watkin added the 'Wynn' to his name because he had inherited the land of the Wynn family. The Wynn family crest included an eagle – and on a Jacobite drinking glass engraved with his name……

….. Sir Watkin has added that eagle.

On the outside East Wall of St. Mary le Strand, two eagles perch above the ouroboros and V – both looking South to France…

The White Rose medal also has a love-knot as part of its design….

……a reference to the Jacobite rallying cry 'Look, Love and Follow'……

St. Mary le Strand is covered with love-knot designs…

47

.....even on its oak pulpit.....

.....and there are 'White Roses' – the name of Sir Watkin's Club – on the ceiling.

Sir Watkin Williams-Wynn seems to have left his calling card all over St. Mary le Strand. He could well be the reason that Gibbs was able to design the Church without a fee, why the two front pillars arrived as an anonymous gift in the 1740s and why the whole building looks so opulent and so stunningly beautiful.

But was St. Mary le Strand 'Masonic'?

At the time the Church was being built, most Masonic meetings in London took place in 'imaginary' temples – small rooms in taverns marked-up with charts and symbols as in the Parisian Lodge illustrated on page 49.

There are still many small rooms in many small taverns along the Strand – and it has been estimated that between 1725 and 1825 – when Freemasonry was at the height of its popularity – over 57 different Lodges held meetings there.

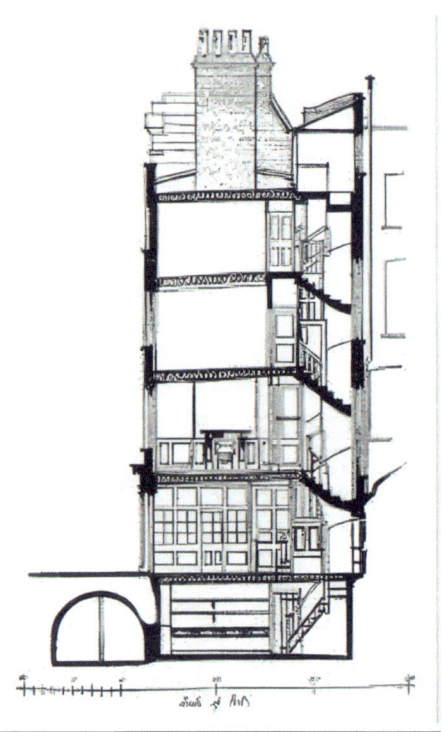

The Goose and Gridiron, site of 'The Grand Lodge' in 1717.

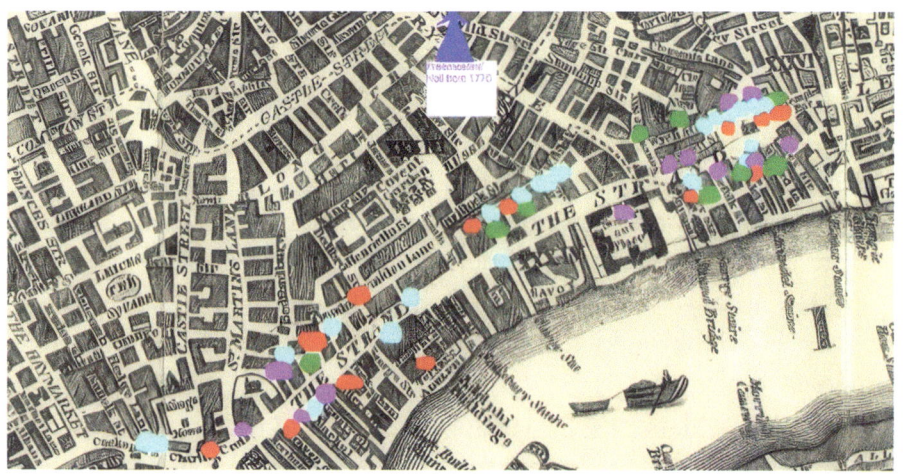

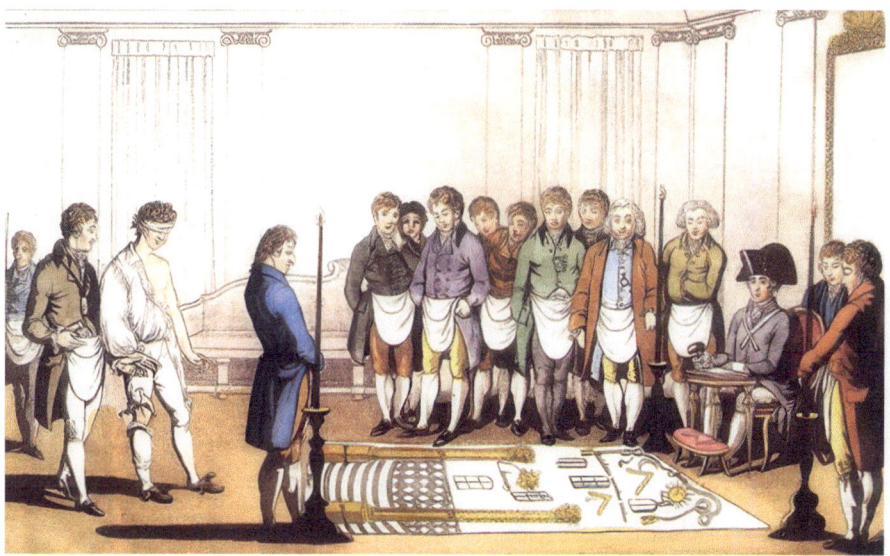

In my home town of Southend-on-Sea – which, like many British seaside towns, has a strong Masonic presence – there are what are called 'Lodges of Instruction' – in which Masonic rites are 'rehearsed' and there are Temples where they are enacted for 'real'.

Were these Strand taverns Lodges of Instruction?

We know the first purpose built Grand Lodge in London was erected in 1775. What did Masons do before that?

Did they, by any chance, use St. Mary le Strand Church?

It may come as a surprise to learn that Churches in Britain had been used for this purpose before.

According to Anderson in his 'Constitutions,' Scottish Masons –

49

who at one point held their rituals in the open air – would retire into monasteries if the weather became inclement.

Both John Aubrey and John Evelyn tell us that Wren was adopted into the Masonic fraternity at St. Paul's Church, Covent Garden, on 18th May 1691. According to Anderson, Wren at that time was re-working Inigo Jones's designs for Hampton Cout for King William – where 'a bright lodge was held during the building'.

Masonic Meetings, it seems, were held in daylight on building sites – with 'tylers' [look-outs] keeping 'cowans' [the uninitiated or unqualified masons] at bay.

There is evidence that this happened at St. Mary le Strand.

On 12th September 1717 the Commission for Building 50 Churches noted that the workmen had been 'guilty of great disorder at Strand church upon finishing of tower, master mason and other master workmen to attend at next meeting'.

On 10th October 1717 the minutes recorded 'Townsend attending was asked to explain disorders at the finishing of tower of Strand church, and charged to try to prevent such disorders in future'.

This placing of the capstone on the tower was a great Masonic ceremony – followed by heavy drinking. Gibbs was to get involved in a similar ceremony four years later when the foundation stone to St. Martin-in-the-Fields – which Gibbs had designed – was levelled. The Masons then toasted 'The King and the Craft' – but this time they went to a tavern.

In 1722 Nathaniel Blackerby – Nicholas Hawksmoor's son-in-law – became the Treasurer of the Commission for Building 50 Churches. He was a leading Freemason and an advocate for the Craft who wrote Masonic Prologues for Drury Lane.

According to Masonic Sources he was the also the Treasurer for St. Mary le Strand, St Clement Danes and St. Martin-in-the Fields – so might well have encouraged Masonic Rites in the Church when it was being built.

Matthew Birkhead – a singer and actor at Drury Lane and a member of The Lodge of Friendship associated with the theatre. -- was given a full Masonic funeral and burial at next door St. Clement Dane's Church early in 1723, following a procession by 'a vast number of Accepted Masons' walking 'two by two in their white aprons'.

Birkhead was the writer of the famous 'Enter'd Aprentice Song' which was, in all likelihood, sung by him, Gibbs and all the other Freemasons at the scenes of 'great disorder' in the Church in 1717:

Masonic Procession in the Strand – by Somerset House – in 1742.

'Then join Hand in Hand

To each other firm stand;

Let's be merry, and put a bright face on

What mortal can boast

So noble a Toast as a Free and an Accepted Mason!'

But were Masonic meetings held at St. Mary le Strand after it was consecrated?

Secret movements leave few traces behind. Sir Watkin Williams-Wynn's wife, for instance, burnt all her husband's papers the night he died.

In recent years, the Masonic movement has become far more open than it was and has given me – a non-Mason – access to its records, many of which are available on line.

1. THE DESIGN OF THE CHURCH

St. Mary le Strand is 'Masonic' by virtue of its very design! Gibbs re-created the Temple of Solomon as described in the Bible – with a porch, winding staircase, inner sanctum, high windows and a Holy of Holies. All of these feature heavily in Masonic practices.

2. THE PORCH.

The Porch of the Temple of Solomon was a place of huge importance to Freemasons as the Craft was said to have originated there. Old plans show that a vault was built beneath the porch of St. Mary le Strand which has now been blocked up. Were rites enacted there?

3. THE WINDING STAIRCASE

The St. Mary le Strand winding stairway is very similar to the one Inigo Jones designed for the Queens' House in Greenwich – the first self-supporting staircase in Britain. The upper part of Jones's staircase is divided into fifteen step sections.

Jones was a Freemason and the Queens' House – with its starburst, tessallated black and white floor and cube hall – might well have been used as a Lodge.

The winding stairway at Chiswick House has fifteen steps. There are 45 steps in the St. Mary le Strand staircase leading up to the gallery – three units of fifteen. Freemasons further divide the fifteen steps into groups of three, five and seven.

This was a memory system – a way of filing knowledge – for people who could not read.

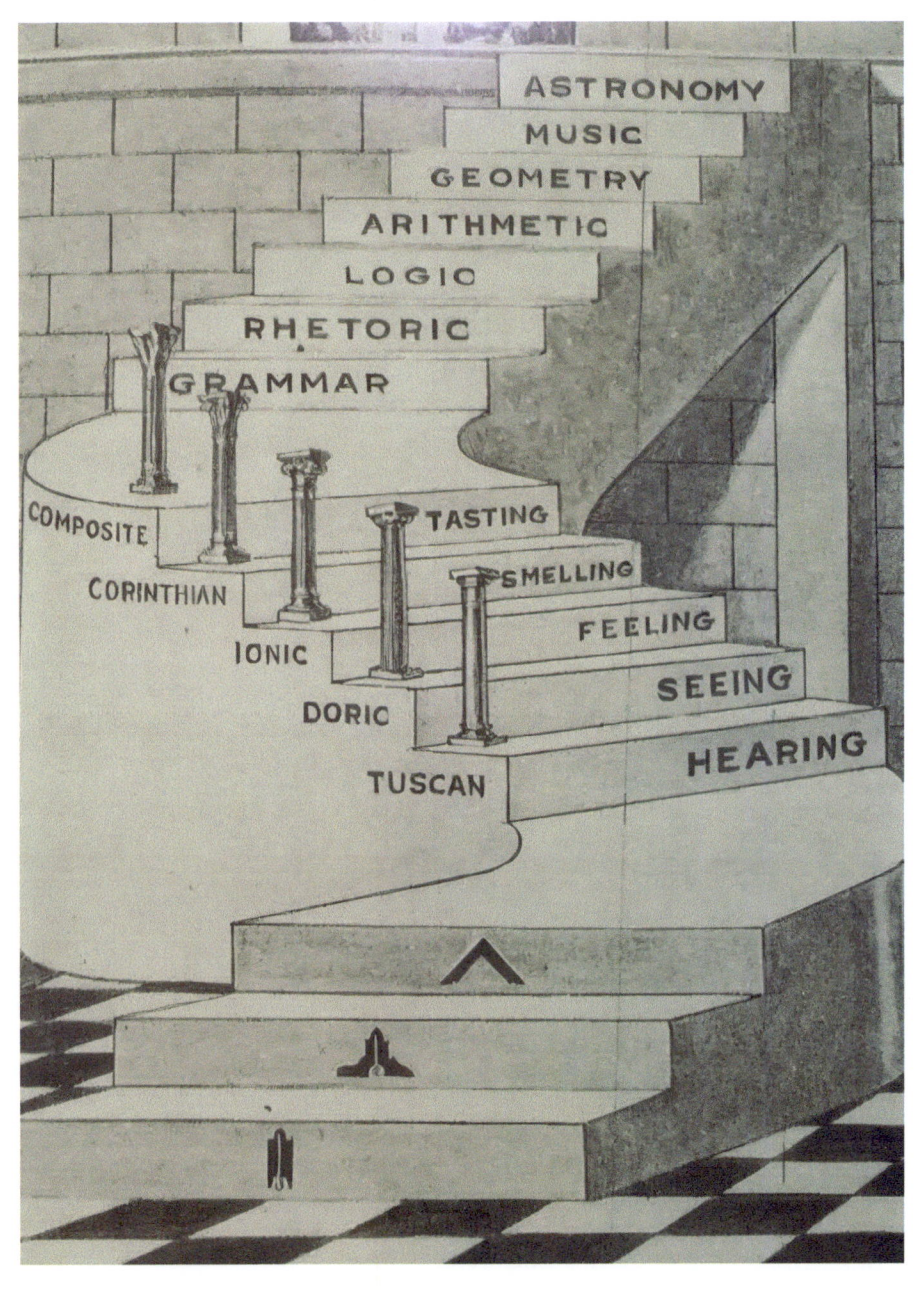

The St. Mary le Strand stairway was clearly built off-site. It doesn't quite fit and bits of it have had to be shaved off.

Staircase at St. Mary le Strand.

Staircase at Queen's House.

This was in compliance with an order from the Commission on 29th July 1714 that 'the masons employed to build the new church in the Strand to prepare their stones ready for setting before they build them on site.'

According to Anderson in his 'Constitutions', King Solomon built his Temple 'by divine Direction, without the noise of Work-men's tools'.

The Hall at Queen's House – a near perfect cube!

This idea makes up part of the ritual of Third Degree Masonry when the Apprentice is asked why he was divested of all metal when he became a Mason.

He replies: 'There was neither the sound of axe or hammer or any other metal tool heard at the building of King Solomon's Temple….All the stones were hewed, squared and numbered in the quarries where they were raised…Every part thereof fitted with an exact nicety, that it had more the resemblance of the handy workmanship of the Supreme Architect of the Universe than of human hands'.

Were the Masons on the Commission (at this date still both Jacobite and Hanoverian) trying to re-create the building of the Temple of Solomon?

It all stopped when Chief Mason Townsend reported to the Commission that it was impracticable to build off-site.

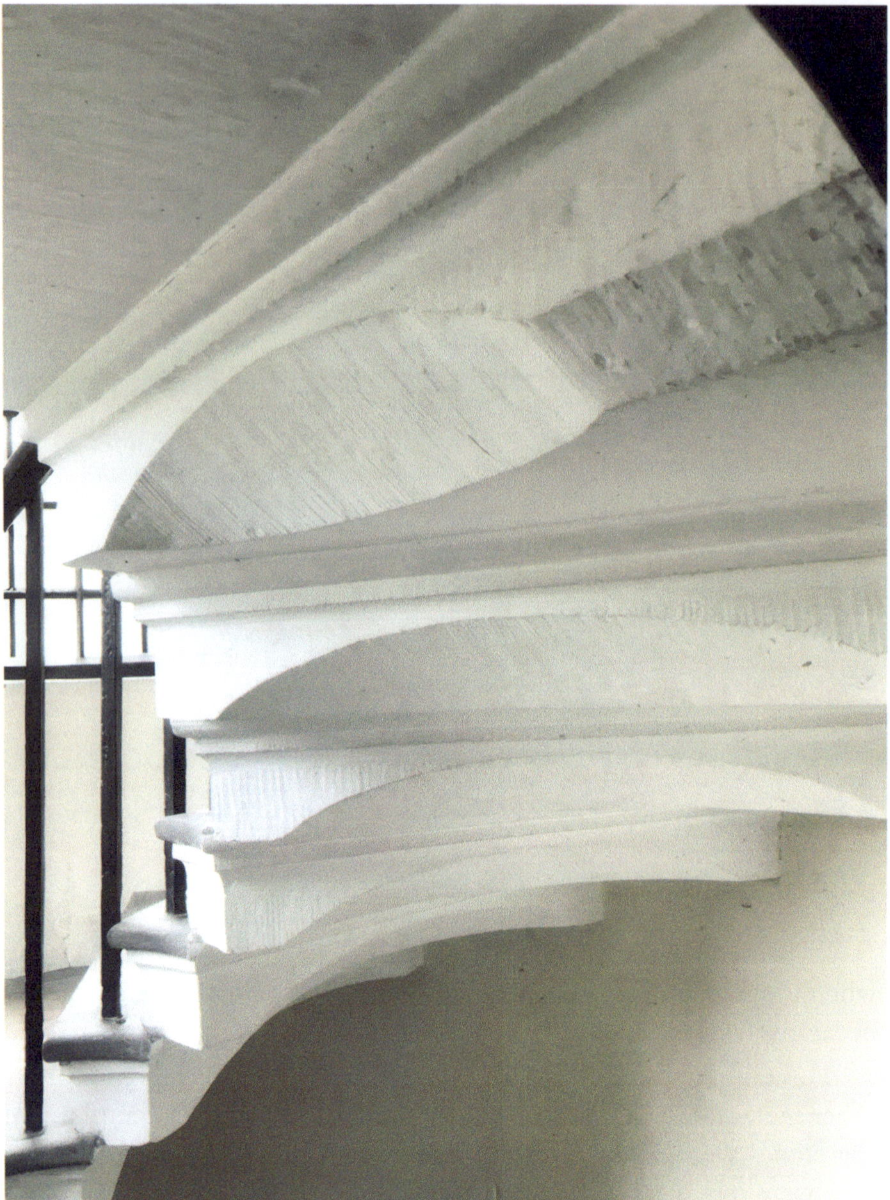

4. THE GRAFFITI IN THE STAIRWELL.

Ritualistically an Apprentice Mason – blindfolded and stripped down – with one slipper off and one on – is led up the stairs by a rope. He wears his white Masonic apron – but with the flap pinned up, the sign that he is an apprentice.

He knocks at the Outer Door of the Inner Chamber, gives the password and grip and is admitted. He then does the same at the Inner Door of the Inner Chamber – he is admitted and his 'hoodwink' removed to blinding light and claps and stamps as he is 'Enlightened'. The flap on his apron is unpinned and lowered now he has been initiated.

Does the graffiti in the stairwell represent the aprons of Apprentice Masons before their initiation?

Did the Muniments Room in the gallery of St. Mary le Strand also double as a Masonic Inner Chamber? It has a lock that can only be opened with three keys, which means three different people must be present to open the door.

This is similar to the famous 'Lokit Kist' of the Aberdeen Masonic lodge [c. 1700] – a box containing the Lodge's 'Mark Book' (the book with Members' names) that also has three keys for the same reasons of security and secrecy.

[Note: The St. Mary le Strand lock is clearly later than the 1720s – but it is likely to be a replacement for a similar three-lock design.]

Another piece of graffiti in the stairway features a gallows.

According to Swift's Grand Mistress of the Freemasons, the gallows was important to Freemasons because it represented letters from the Hebrew language.

'Cheth and Thau are shaped like two standing gallowses, of two legs each'.

'When two masons accost each other, the one cries Cheth and the other answers Thau; signifying that they would sooner be hanged on the gallows, than divulge the secret.'

Swift might be writing satire here, but the gallows certainly played a large part in Masonic Rituals in London in the 1720s.....

………employing 'ladders in darkened rooms'…..

Upstairs passageway and room beneath the steeple in St. Mary le Strand Church.

And in the Royal Arch Degree, a Knight of the Red Cross swears that if he violates the Laws of the Order he binds himself 'under no less penalty than having my house torn down, the timbers thereof set up, and I hanged thereon....'

5. THE INNER SANCTUM

(i) The High Windows in the Church follow a description of the Temple of Solomon in the Bible (1 Kings, 6:4). Gibbs claimed that St. Mary le Strand 'consists of two orders in the upper of which the lights are placed: the wall in the lower being solid to keep out noises in the street.'

In reality, having the windows in the Church high up makes little difference to the sound penetrating the Church. But it does provide for extraordinary beams of light entering at different angles at different times of day.

Light is an essential symbol to Freemasons, who move from darkness to light in the course of their initiation and training. Also, having windows high up makes it difficult for 'Cowans' to see in.

The Revd. Peter Babington, the Priest-in-Charge at St. Mary le Strand.

Also the light from the gallery window floods the High Altar mid afternoon…..

(ii) The current floor to the St. Mary le Strand was laid in Victorian times – but there remain in the north and south aisles the original tessellated flooring, characteristic of Masonic Lodges.

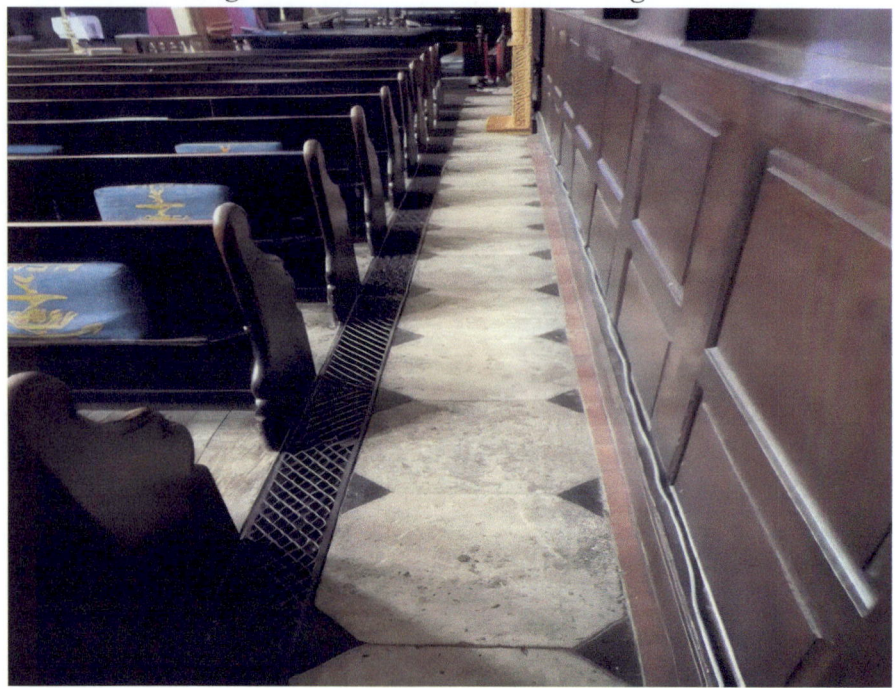

(iii) The ceiling of the Inner Sanctum is curved and was, experts think, originally blue – as it is in Gibbs's design for Wimpole Hall….

In the words of Royal Arch Masonry, 'Blue is an emblem of universal friendship and benevolence, and instructs us, that in the mind of a Mason those virtues should be as expansive as the blue arch of Heaven itself.'

Scottish Masons, it will be remembered, originally held their meetings in the open air.

Many Masonic Lodges have curved blue 'sky' ceilings. This one is from eighteenth century America....

......and this was designed by Sir John Soanes in the late 1820s.....

In Royal Arch Masonry, three groups of three form a 'Living Arch' by grasping each others wrists and raising their arms.

At initiation, 'Apprentice Knights' have to crawl, hoodwinked and tethered, on their hands and knees beneath the living arch which then collapses on top of them and crushes them.

64

To be a Royal Arch Mason you had to be a practising Christian and the Masonic injunction in this ceremony is reminiscent of the Magnificat:

'Let them enter under a Living Arch, and remember to stoop low, for he that humbleth himself shall be exalted.'

In another rite, the Knights form an 'Arch of Steel….their swords elevated above their heads, forming a cross, each placing his left hand upon the other's right shoulder'.

(iv) On the 16th May 1717 the Commission approved Gibbs's plan 'for the pewing of the Strand Church, except that the aisle be ten foot wide'. We don't know if the Commission were increasing or decreasing Gibbs's original aisle width – but it is far wider than the Victorian pews are now.

There had been the purge of Jacobites from the Commission by this time – but there were still many Hanoverian Masons on the Commission. The wide aisles would be perfect for processions and for the acting out of the central story of Third Degree Masonry – the murder, by three 'Cowans', of Harim Abiff – the Architect of the Temple of Solomon – because he refused to divulge the Mason Word to them.

6. THE VAULTS.

The vaults of St. Mary le Strand are a mystery.

On 22nd April 1714 the Commission for Building 50 Churches suddenly came up with an extraordinary change of plan. Every church – including the ones already half-built like Greenwich – should be 'vaulted under the pavements'. The surveyors were asked to estimate how much extra this would cost.

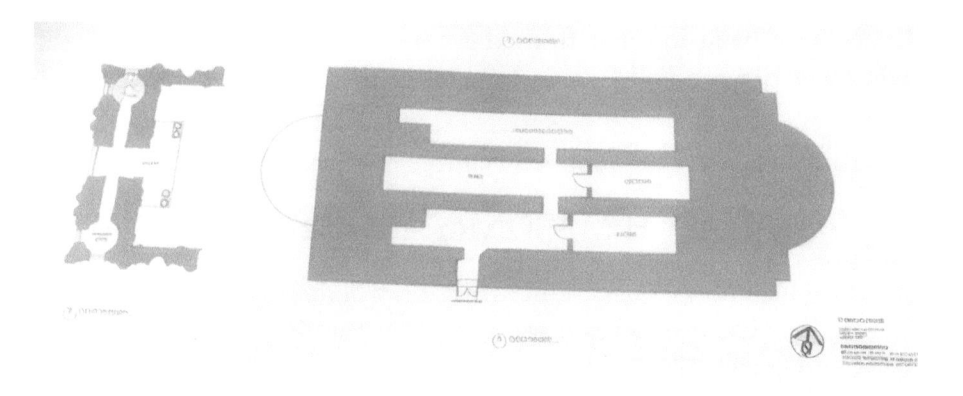

The Commission was insistent that no bodies were to be buried in the vaults – so what were the vaults for?

There are three vaults beneath the flooring of St. Mary le Strand *(shown in the plan on page 65)* which clearly lead into a space beneath the High Altar – but these passages have been bricked up.

Also, to add to the confusion, many skeletons were placed in the vaults in the early nineteenth century. Templar Masons often employed skulls and crossbones in their rites as they brooded, Hamlet-like, on their mortality. In one rite, a Knight drinks wine from the top of a skull – swearing that if he ever divulges the secrets of the Templars he will take on, as well as his own, the sins of the man whose skull he is holding.

This ritual forms the opening sequence in Dan Brown's novel, 'The Lost Symbol'....

By a bizarre freak, the top of a human skull has been discovered on a shelf in the vault – probably put there in the nineteenth century – but still worth a D.N.A test!

Excavations are planned. But in the meantime the most obvious question to ask is:

'Were the vaults used for Masonic Rituals?'

THIRD DEGREE MASONRY

In Third Degree Masonry the 'body' of Harim Abiff is buried by the Cowans in a shallow grave. It is discovered when a sprig of acacia is dislodged and then buried with full honour in the vault of the Holy of Holies in the Temple of Solomon.

If excavations under the High Altar find a hollow space, the 'body' could have been lowered from the apse down into a vault. Probably Matthew Birkhead's Masonic Funeral at St. Clement Danes in 1722 followed this rite.

Vaults play an even more crucial role in Royal Arch Masonry.

ROYAL ARCH MASONRY – THE SCOTTISH RITE

No-one knows for certain when or where Royal Arch Masonry began. Jane Clark believes it was created at the time of the Restoration of King Charles II – but there is growing evidence that it goes back, as much of Masonry seems to do, to the reign of James VI. Language and imagery – and even thought – in Royal Arch Masonry is very similar to William Shakespeare's plays – particularly 'Macbeth'.

King James built his own Temple of Solomon – together with a vault – at Stirling Castle in 1594 to celebrate the baptism of his son, Prince Henry. Gibbs was Surveyor of the Castle – and the design of the arched entry to the Temple has clearly influenced the design of St. Mary le Strand.

At Prince Harry's baptism, King James dressed as a Knight of Malta. He also staged battles between the Templars and the Turks – one of the central motifs of Royal Arch Masonry.

Legend has it that Robert the Bruce gave shelter to the Knights Templar in Scotland when they were persecuted in Europe – and in gratitude they fought with him against the English at Bannockburn.

Legend also has it that Bonnie Dundee revived the Order of the Temple when he was fighting the Government Forces at Killiekrankie.

He was said to have been wearing a Templar Cross beneath his breast plate when he was shot.

But what we do know for certain is that the Earl of Mar was made Grand Master of the Order of the Temple by James III in 1722 – and that Bonnie Prince Charlie himself inherited the title in Holyrood House in 1745.

Of this gathering the Duke of Perth wrote to Lord Ogilvy that 'it is truly a proud thing to see our Prince in the Palace of his fathers with all the best blood in Scotland around him. Our noble Prince looked most gallant in the white robe of the Order and took his profession like a worthy Knight.'

A Knight of the Order of the Temple.

Legend also has it that the Knights Templar brought fabulous treasures and sacred objects with them from Jerusalem – and how they discovered them forms the basis of the most demanding rite of Royal Arch Masonry.

In one of the rites the 'Knights' discover a hollow-sounding rock in the floor of the ruins of the Temple of Solomon. They remove it by means of an attached metal ring and discover a dark, secret vault – filled with rubbish and noxious air.

Lots are cast, a Knight has ropes tied round his waist and is lowered into the vault, either by hand or by a winch. He has a smaller rope in his hand that he can pull on if he is overcome by fumes or exhaustion – and with a spade and pickaxe he searches for treasure. If he is in luck, he pulls on his rope and emerges, triumphant, with the Ark of the Covenant.

The High Altar at St. Mary le Strand was originally in the form of the Ark of the Covenant, perhaps a reference to this rite. *(See p. 69.)*

Another rite – enacted by 'The Knights of the

The Ark of the Covenant – which formed part of the original design of the High Altar at St.Mary le Strand.

Ninth Arch' – is set at the time of King Solomon himself. It has the same actions and narrative – but this time the treasure sought is 'the brilliant triangle' – 'the most precious jewel of Masonry' – 'a triangular plate of gold, richly adorned' – the Delta of Enoch.

The Delta, as visitors to St. Mary le Strand will know, features prominently in the Church's apse....

It had originally been vouchsafed to Enoch – the great grandfather of Noah – who had been transported by angels to a high mountain in the heavens where he saw the Sacred Triangle – carved with strange letters he did not understand. He was then transported through the bowels of the earth down to a secret vault where he saw the Delta again – without the letters – and he was told to carve on it the Hebrew name for God.

At St Mary le Strand the Delta has the first syllable of that name – 'Jah' – which is also the first syllable of the tri-syllabic Royal Arch 'Mason Word'.

Enoch hid the Delta in a Sacred Vault because, with his 'Second Sight', he foresaw that the world would be overwhelmed with a flood...

The vaults at St. Mary le Strand would be perfect for this rite – it even has an old spade....

……and rubble……..

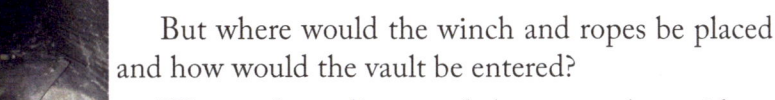

But where would the winch and ropes be placed and how would the vault be entered?

We may have discovered the answer by accident. Last year architects were working on the stone flaming urns on the roof – many of which have fallen with time and rust….

……when, to their amazement, they discovered, by camera, a hidden room and stairway above the South Vestry.

There was a wooden structure above the window that could well have been a cradle for a winch – and the vestry below has a central hole through which a rope could be fed.

Excavations will reveal if one of the stone slabs on the floor could be removed for entry to the crypt.

Chiswick House – although it's not been commented on before – has exactly the same set up. An upstairs door opening onto to a gaping drop…..

………to the cellar below…….

......which could well have doubled as a round chapel for Templar Knight ceremonies.

We are told that there used to be a pulley system there to winch up wine. But that system could have also been used to winch down Knights....

And what of the secret staircase in St. Mary le Strand?

It appears to lead to a bridge corridor across the apse behind the Hanoverian Crest, then, perhaps, down another stairway, to the North Vestry.

Until we can access the area, we cannot know for certain but, it would seem you had to 'stoop low' through the brick arch to make your way across the apse.

You certainly had to 'duck' when you entered or left the staircase at the west end of the church....

The roof over the east stairway system – shown on the right of this photo – is flat….

This could well be another Royal Arch rite – where you move from light into darkness and back into light again – possibly blind-folded, tied up and pulled by a rope - humbling yourself by stooping beneath a Brick Arch so you can be 'exalted'.

And that 'exaltation' would have been built into your journey. You might have to 'stoop low' and fumble your way across the apse – behind the triangular Hanoverian Crest – but you would also be, like Enoch, up in the Heavens, way above the High Altar and even above the Delta

And after these humiliations you would be granted your 'enlightenment' – the sight of a burning bush….

..... an effect created by an 'inflamed urn'.

Could this be why there seems to be soot on the walls of the hidden chamber as well as the vaults, in places far away from the Victorian boiler?

And why the church was originally decorated with no fewer than forty flaming urns?

.......including one above the High 'Ark of the Covenant' Altar.

Let's hope the planned excavations in the Church will give us the answers to at least some of these questions.

POSTSCRIPT

David Hume – the Scottish philosopher and historian – claimed in a letter he wrote on 10th February 1773 to Sir John Pringle that Bonnie Prince Charlie had secretly visited London in 1753 and had abjured his Roman Catholicism at the 'The new church in the Strand'.

Hume didn't go to live in London till the1760s and he got the date wrong: it was 1750. Prince Charlie was planning another rebellion. Although the Battle of Culloden had been a blood bath from which the Young Pretender had fled, he had done well before that. Many people thought that if he had marched on London – as he wanted to do – he would have won. King George II had packed his bags and was ready to go.

The new plan was to infiltrate London with Jacobite troops – all staying separately at different taverns and boarding houses – and then to storm the Tower of London and murder – or deport – the whole Hanoverian Royal Family.

Hume's letter to Sir John Pringle was published, after Hume's death, in the Gentleman's Magazine of January 1788 – and an anonymous contributer challenged this, claiming that the church where this happened was in Gray's Inn.

That is probably the case. But we do know that Bonnie Prince Charlie was at Lady Primrose's house in Essex Street on 16th September – a three to four minute walk from St. Mary le Strand – and that William King visited him.

King, as we have seen, was one of Gibbs's closest friends – and had just spent ten years working with him on the Radcliffe Library (now 'Camera') in Oxford.

To my mind it is inconceivable that King didn't take Charles Stuart across the road to see his beloved colleague's masterpiece.....

A Bust of Gibbs which is thought he gifted to Alexander Pope.